APPOINTMENT WITH A HIGHWIRE LADY

Russell Davis

BROADWAY PLAY PUBLISHING INC
New York
www.broadwayplaypublishing.com
info@broadwayplaypublishing.com

APPOINTMENT WITH A HIGHWIRE LADY
© Copyright 2003 by Russell Davis

Cover art by Kat O'Brien
First printing: September 2007
I S B N: 978-0-88145-355-3

Book design: Marie Donovan
Word processing: Microsoft Word
Typographic controls: Ventura Publisher
Typeface: Palatino
Printed and bound in the U S A

APPOINTMENT WITH A HIGHWIRE LADY was produced at Alice's Fourth Floor, Theater Row, N Y C, 30 January-1 March 1992; Long Wharf Theater, Stage II, New Haven, CT, 13 December 1991-19 January 1992; and Ensemble Studio Theater, N Y C, 22 March-22 April 1991 (workshop production), with the following cast and creative contributors:

RICHARD . . . . Victor Slezak
LOUISE . . . . Jayne Atkinson
CARLA . . . . Suzanne Shepherd

Director . . . . Michael Mantell
Scenic designer . . . . Michael Francis Moody
   (Long Wharf: David Fletcher, *set coordination & props*)
Lighting designer . . . . Michael Francis Moody
                                  (Long Wharf: Jay Strevey)
Costume designer . . . . David Sawaryn
   (Long Wharf: Patricia M Risser, *costume coordination*)
Production stage manager . . . . Sally Plass
                               (Long Wharf: Tom Aberger)

There was an earlier workshop production at New York Stage & Film, Vassar College, Poughkeepsie, NY in June 1990. The cast and creative contributors were:

RICHARD ....Zeljko Ivanek
LOUISE .... Frances McDormand
CARLA ....Carla Belver

Director .... Abigail Adams
Stage manager .... Patricia Saraniero

There were readings and development work at New Dramatists, N Y C; Playwrights Theater of New Jersey, Madison; Lehigh University, Bethlehem, PA; Circle Repertory Company, N Y C.

CHARACTERS & SETTING

RICHARD SKELLEY, *a young man in trouble*
LOUISE WICK, *a young woman who visits him*
CARLA UKMAR, *an old lady in disrepair*

A room in a state psychiatric center. There are several chairs, a linoleum floor, and a clock on one wall. A painting, or print, of a little stream flowing through the woods is on another wall. Otherwise the room is empty. The door to this room has bars. On the floor downstage are shadows cast by the bars in windows. The walls to this room are pale green, though these walls might not be visible. The painting and clock might just hang in the air.

Time: some years ago

Darkling I listen; and, for many a time
I have been half in love with easeful Death,
Called him soft names in many a muséd rhyme,
To take into the air my quiet breath;
Now more than ever seems it rich to die,
To cease upon the midnight with no pain,
While thou art pouring forth thy soul abroad
In such an ecstasy!
—John Keats, *Ode to a Nightingale*

ACT ONE

(A room with pale green walls. RICHARD *sits in a chair underneath the clock.* LOUISE *enters. She looks at* RICHARD *who pays no attention. She comes into the room. She carries a shoulder bag. Pause)*

LOUISE: Is this where you sit?

(Pause. RICHARD *looks at* LOUISE.)

LOUISE: You like to sit here?

(Pause. RICHARD *looks away.)*

LOUISE: I was told you like to sit here. You sit all day. In the visiting room.

(No response)

LOUISE: They told me you don't talk to your visitors.

(No response)

LOUISE: This isn't much of a room to visit.

*(*RICHARD *leans stiffly back in his chair. He closes his eyes.* LOUISE *looks at the clock above where* RICHARD *sits. The clock doesn't work. She puts aside her shoulder bag.* CARLA *appears at the door. Pause)*

CARLA: You're probably going to have to wait.

LOUISE: Excuse me?

CARLA: That's what I do.

LOUISE: You wait?

CARLA: Yeah. I wait. *(She steps into the room.)* You a friend?

LOUISE: Yes. I am.

CARLA: An old friend?

LOUISE: Well, from before. Yes.

CARLA: I'm new. A new friend.

LOUISE: Uh huh.

CARLA: A couple of weeks old, that's all. We like each other. What do you think of that? We met in here.

LOUISE: I think that's good.

CARLA: Hm?

LOUISE: I said, Good. It's good you're friends.

CARLA: I don't think so.

LOUISE: Pardon?

CARLA: What kind of old friend could think it's good to meet a new friend like me? *(Pause)* Those are very nice. You have very nice shoes.

LOUISE: Oh?

CARLA: Probably you have pretty feet in there.

LOUISE: In my shoes?

CARLA: Yeah. It takes a pretty foot to get into a shoe like that.

LOUISE: *(Looking down)* No, these are very simple.

CARLA: I don't think I could fit into them. That's not so simple.

LOUISE: Well, they seem the same size.

CARLA: No, they don't fit. I have to put my feet in slippers.

LOUISE: What for?

CARLA: Because they don't fit in shoes. They have bumps on them. You can't put bumps like these in shoes.

(CARLA *takes a slipper off. She shows* LOUISE *her foot.*)

LOUISE: *(startled)* What happened to your foot?

CARLA: Just some bumps. That's all.

LOUISE: I'm sorry about your foot.

CARLA: It's okay. You don't have to be kind.

LOUISE: I'm not kind.

CARLA: No, somebody previous used this foot. That's all. This was never a fresh foot. (*Steps out of her other slipper. She regards both feet.*) Yeah. I think my feet are hand-me-downs. Or else, I think more than one person have been walking on these feet. A bunch of other people. They must walk on them at night. These people when I'm sleeping. Because every morning I wake up, and I look down. And I think, oh, boy, they look sore. They must be at it again. Whoever is using my feet. This morning I looked down and I thought a dancing student. I hope a dancing student is using them. To help her leap, keep on her toes. But I don't think so. I think it's just a fighter. Somebody fighting now in the mountains, and her boots are broken. Because of the enemy. The enemy is somewhere. Trying to make one of those things. What do you call those things? A beachhead? Do you think they are using my feet at night to make a beachhead?

LOUISE: I'm sorry. I don't know.

CARLA: No, incursion. Beachhead is for the ocean. Somebody is trying to make an incursion.

LOUISE: Yes?

CARLA: Yeah, with my feet. I think so. *(Steps back into her slippers)* Anyway. I can't be like you. I can't fit my feet back into shoes.

(CARLA takes a chair. She sits across from RICHARD.)

CARLA: He looks like he's on a ledge to me. His feet are on a ledge.

LOUISE: What ledge?

CARLA: I don't know. Just a little ledge.

(CARLA regards RICHARD.)

CARLA: I used to fall asleep like that. Lean back and sleep. Straight up. At attention.

LOUISE: You don't do that now?

CARLA: No. I'm relaxed now. *(Pause)* The clock doesn't work. On the wall. Did you notice?

LOUISE: Yes. I saw.

CARLA: Yeah. Might be a long wait. *(Pause)* Do you have other friends out there? Lots of friends outside in your life?

LOUISE: I think so.

CARLA: Do they change? These friends.

LOUISE: Is there a turnover, you mean?

CARLA: No, the same people. They change?

LOUISE: Sure. They change.

CARLA: How about you? Did you change?

LOUISE: Yes. I've changed.

CARLA: Are you happy now?

LOUISE: I guess so. Sure.

CARLA: Uh huh. I changed too.

LOUISE: I can imagine.

CARLA: I never used to be here. *(Pause)* Tell me a change. I want to know a change in you.

LOUISE: One change?

CARLA: Yeah. Tell me.

LOUISE: A change, okay. My exuberance.

CARLA: Hm?

LOUISE: I'm not as exuberant, I think.

CARLA: Exuberant?

LOUISE: Uh huh. That's a change.

CARLA: You don't do that now?

LOUISE: No, I'm more disciplined now. Circumspect.

CARLA: Uh huh.

LOUISE: Mature, I think.

CARLA: I used to be exuberant too.

LOUISE: Did you?

CARLA: Yeah, I liked it. Exuberant.

LOUISE: It's nice.

CARLA: My friends too. They were exuberant.

LOUISE: Yes, I know. Mine too.

CARLA: You had exuberant friends?

LOUISE: I think so. I think that's what I remember.

CARLA: He was exuberant?

LOUISE: Richard?

CARLA: Yeah, our friend. He was an exuberant friend once upon a time?

LOUISE: He was. Very exuberant.

CARLA: That's good. I thought so.

LOUISE: You did, huh?

CARLA: Yeah. I could see it.

LOUISE: Where?

CARLA: In his looks. When he looks, he looks like he's trying to remember something.

LOUISE: No, he looks blank.

CARLA: No, I think it could be exuberant. Something in that look. Could be what you and I remember too. *(Pause)* Anyway. Our friend is okay. They like to keep him separate. That's all. They like it if he stays in this room.

LOUISE: Who likes?

CARLA: The nurses and clean-up people. They think it's better.

LOUISE: No, they told me he likes to sit here. They didn't say anything about keeping him separate.

CARLA: He thinks it's better too. There's a man in the dayroom he likes to hit.

LOUISE: Richard hits a man?

CARLA: I'd hit him too.

LOUISE: Why, what does he do, this man?

CARLA: Ask him. Ask our friend here about Malcolm Cribbs.

LOUISE: Okay.

CARLA: Yeah, you ask him. When he talks. Malcolm Cribbs.

LOUISE: Okay, I will.

(CARLA comes downstage. She looks out through a window.)

CARLA: Do you have a car?

LOUISE: Yes, I do.

CARLA: I don't see it.

(LOUISE *comes downstage. She looks out another window.*)

LOUISE: It must be parked around the side.

CARLA: What's it like?

LOUISE: It's just a beat-up car.

CARLA: Yeah? It's not big and shiny new?

LOUISE: No, it's old. I keep things in it.

(*They look out the windows.*)

CARLA: The first time our friend had a visitor, I came to this window and I could see a big car. Very shiny new, and fast. And I asked him the name of his car, this visitor, he had red raving hair. And he said, Jaguar. He called it, Jaguar. (*Pause*) Do you know the man with red hair and the Jaguar?

LOUISE: Yes, I do.

CARLA: That's your friend?

LOUISE: He didn't always have a Jaguar.

CARLA: Did you spend time together? With this man?

LOUISE: No, we don't.

(*Pause*)

CARLA: My name is Carla Ukmar.

LOUISE: I'm Louise. Hello.

CARLA: My mother was from Italy.

LOUISE: Yes?

CARLA: But I am from Rumania. I was a young girl there. And then I met a man from Croatia. And so I became a young woman in Croatia. In the mountains. I was exuberant there, uh huh. So exuberant I thought I could change all the things out there. My friends and I. We wanted to make some changes. Yeah. We expected it. Expected this old world to go away. Make a new one.

LOUISE: That must have felt nice.

CARLA: I think so. I think it was nice.

LOUISE: What changes did you hope to make?

CARLA: Hm?

LOUISE: What exactly did you change?

CARLA: I don't know. Everybody I know was scattered.

LOUISE: Scattered where?

CARLA: It's okay. I'm relaxed now.

LOUISE: When was this?

CARLA: He's looking at you.

LOUISE: What?

CARLA: Our friend has opened his eyes. And now he's looking.

(Pause)

LOUISE: He's staring.

CARLA: No, I think he wants to remember. (Goes to the door)

CARLA: Don't forget to ask about Malcolm Cribbs. He'll talk if you mention Malcolm Cribbs.

LOUISE: Okay.

CARLA: Good. (Exits)

(RICHARD continues to look at LOUISE. LOUISE sits down in a chair. Pause)

LOUISE: I hear you won't talk.

(No response)

LOUISE: Not to visitors anyway. Those who visit.
The only people you talk to these days seem to be in
this hospital. You seem to have forgotten about the rest
of us. *(Pause)* Harris visited. Several times. He told me.
Harris is the one who told me you were here. He told
me yesterday. Called me up. I had no idea. And he told
me you haven't said a word to him. Or your father.
Anybody from before. People just come in and give
you speeches. Because you won't talk to them. *(Pause)*
Harris says you're indigent. Somehow you've become
indigent. Destitute. No insurance. And so now this is
a state institution. You're in a state institution. And I
don't care what you feel about your father, what you
can't remember, the least you could do is let them put
you somewhere else. Or Harris. He could put you.
(Pause) You want to talk about Malcolm Cribbs? *(Pause)*
There's a man in there called Malcolm Cribbs.
Evidently you hit him. That woman, the friendly
woman, Carla, she says so. *(Pause)* I guess you're not
talking. *(Gets up from her chair. She comes downstage.
She looks out through a window.)*

RICHARD: I can talk.

(LOUISE turns. She comes back upstage. She sits down again.)

LOUISE: My name is Louise.

(No response)

LOUISE: Louise. Do you remember Louise? *(Pause)*
Your name is Richard.

RICHARD: I know my name is Richard.

(Pause)

LOUISE: I've come to visit. Did they tell you? *(Pause)*
The staff. Did they say I was coming to visit?

RICHARD: Yes.

LOUISE: But you don't know who I am?

RICHARD: No. I didn't.

LOUISE: And nothing looks familiar?

RICHARD: No.

(Pause)

LOUISE: I'm visiting anyway. *(Pause)* I'm sorry. I seem angry. Probably hurt. I shouldn't feel at all hurt. Considering what's happened to you. But I think it upsets me, screws me up, because I think I told you long ago this could happen. I knew deep down long ago you weren't interested. That there was something in you that was simply not interested in living past a certain point in your life. And therefore that's how you behaved. As if you weren't going to be around after a certain point. And it makes me, a little bit mad, because it attracted me so much, screwed me up so much, and I think it was the hardest thing I ever had to do was to get out of the way of how you weren't going to be around after a certain point. And I did. I got out of the way. And it feels terrible now. It feels years later you stepped off a building or something. You finally let certain things lapse.

Because it's exactly like you fell off some terrible height, and you didn't intend this, I'm sure you didn't, but you've landed. And probably you'll never again ever be anything like what you used to be. *(Pause)* And I think that's a terrible thing to give to the people you know. *(Pause)* Or used to know. *(Gets up. She comes back downstage. She looks out.)*

RICHARD: *(Impressed)* You're Louise?

LOUISE: Yes, I am.

RICHARD: Louise who?

LOUISE: Wick.

RICHARD: Louise Wick.

LOUISE: That's right.

(Pause)

RICHARD: I'm sorry I hurt you. Louise Wick.

LOUISE: That's okay. You're hurt yourself.

RICHARD: I'm not so hurt.

LOUISE: Believe me. I think you're hurt.

(Pause)

RICHARD: Do I look hurt?

LOUISE: No, actually.

RICHARD: I don't look hurt?

LOUISE: I think you look younger.

(Pause)

RICHARD: You look younger too.

LOUISE: Thank you.

RICHARD: Younger than all the people here.

LOUISE: I imagine so. They look pretty beaten.
Pretty forgotten.

(Pause)

RICHARD: You want me to get out?

LOUISE: Yes, I do.

RICHARD: You want me to remember? And believe the
things I did? Those stories?

LOUISE: You don't believe the things you did?

RICHARD: I don't know.

LOUISE: What don't you believe? Tell me something you
don't believe and I'll tell if it's true.

(Pause)

RICHARD: My father is a manufacturer?

LOUISE: Yes. He is.

RICHARD: An important manufacturer?

LOUISE: Yes.

RICHARD: My mother is dead?

LOUISE: Yes.

RICHARD: Those are my parents?

LOUISE: Yes.

(Pause)

RICHARD: I think it's a good day today to have a visitor. Probably the best day so far. Because it seems to me there are days I've sat here, whole days, and I can't remember a thing. Can't feel it. And the next thing I know they're taking me away to bed. Try again tomorrow. And for a while they tried to make me stay in the dayroom. With everybody else. They wanted me in there. But I think they've stopped trying that. I think they understand I don't know how to do that. I don't know how to be in a dayroom right now. And so they let me sit here. In this chair. I like this chair. Because it is all alone off by itself. And that's what I want. I want this chair. Because if I can sit still in this chair, very still, then I think I will hear something. I will hear something probably clear. In the distance. *(Pause)* Do you feel that?

LOUISE: Something clear in the distance?

RICHARD: That you better sit still.

LOUISE: I think so.

RICHARD: Sit still. And listen.

LOUISE: Uh huh. I have.

RICHARD: It's like praying. I think.

LOUISE: What is?

RICHARD: Praying. How hard I sit still. *(Pause)*
This is the first time I've seen you here?

LOUISE: That's right.

(Pause)

RICHARD: I'm glad you came.

(LOUISE *takes a seat. Pause)*

RICHARD: Do you like it here?

LOUISE: Excuse me?

RICHARD: How do you like visiting here?

LOUISE: I don't.

RICHARD: You live somewhere better?

LOUISE: Yes, I do. I live somewhere better.

(Pause)

RICHARD: You asked me about Malcolm Cribbs.
I heard you.

LOUISE: I know. He's somebody you hit.

RICHARD: I've hit him. Yes.

LOUISE: Why?

RICHARD: You don't think I should?

LOUISE: Well, I don't know him.

RICHARD: I don't like to hit him.

LOUISE: No, I'm sure you don't.

RICHARD: I hit Malcolm Cribbs because according to
him our lives are like the universe. They scatter and
spread out. All the events keep getting farther and
farther from each other. The memories. Just spread out.

Accelerate. Till we get to the end, the outer reaches, and we're so thin and spread out and that's it. We have to die. Because there's nothing left that can handle the distances between the events in our lives.

That is what Malcolm Cribbs has to say about life. When it is normal. But he also thinks he is an expert when it is not normal. He has told me the reverse of this theory of losing gradual focus and dying. He has said there is an opposite. There are some of us who don't die. We don't spread out. Which is a black hole. We are like a black hole. All events happen so fast, we don't know how to put distance between them, they happen too fast, and so they pile up on top of each other. They jam all together until you are confronted with this big black ball, this thing with no handles in it, this concentration of memory, time is bent, space, and this thing drags you in and you accelerate, you keep going in, you keep crushing, until you smash right inside. *(Pause)* That is why I hit Malcolm Cribbs. Because he makes me think I am a thing nobody can untangle. Or do anything about. Like death. People ignore me, like death, to get on with their lives. *(Pause)* What did we used to do together?

LOUISE: You and I?

RICHARD: Yes.

LOUISE: I was your girlfriend.

(Pause)

RICHARD: You were my girlfriend?

LOUISE: Yes.

RICHARD: How serious a girlfriend?

LOUISE: Very serious.

RICHARD: I can't imagine that.

LOUISE: Why not?

RICHARD: You look too smart, believe me, to be my girlfriend.

LOUISE: No, evidently, I wasn't.

RICHARD: You weren't smart?

LOUISE: Not in this case.

RICHARD: You're not still my girlfriend?

LOUISE: No. I'm not.

RICHARD: I'm sorry.

LOUISE: I'm sorry too.

RICHARD: What decided you to leave me?

LOUISE: I thought you were dangerous.

RICHARD: Excuse me?

LOUISE: I thought it was dangerous. To stay with you.

RICHARD: In what way, dangerous?

(Pause)

LOUISE: Can we do something first?

RICHARD: Yes?

LOUISE: Can we do something we used to do?

RICHARD: What's that?

(LOUISE reaches over. She takes RICHARD's hand. She holds it.)

LOUISE: You don't remember this? Holding hands.

RICHARD: I don't. No.

LOUISE: Do you think you might?

RICHARD: I want to. Yes.

LOUISE: Okay, then.

RICHARD: I want to remember you. I want to start.

LOUISE: Good. I'm glad you want to. *(Pause)* Tell me. What have people told you? Can you tell me some of the things, Harris, for example, has told you?

(Pause)

RICHARD: He showed me pictures.

LOUISE: Uh huh.

RICHARD: Lots of pictures.

LOUISE: What did you think? Of these pictures?

RICHARD: I didn't remember them.

LOUISE: But you agree they were you? They looked like you?

RICHARD: It was me. Yes. I kicked a ball.

LOUISE: Uh huh.

RICHARD: A couple of pictures like that. Kicking soccer balls.

LOUISE: Playing soccer, right.

RICHARD: And I saw a house. A very big house.

LOUISE: Uh huh.

RICHARD: And I saw myself younger in that house. With a father.

LOUISE: And what did you think?

RICHARD: I thought it looked pretty nice.

LOUISE: Uh huh. Did you want to go back?

RICHARD: I don't think so. It made no sense.

LOUISE: The house didn't?

RICHARD: I don't know. I saw another picture. Pictures where I had a helmet.

LOUISE: Yes?

RICHARD: And boots. There were motorcycles.

LOUISE: Right.

RICHARD: People on motorcycles. In the middle of a racing field. Do you know these people?

LOUISE: No. They were later.

RICHARD: I raced motorcycles later?

LOUISE: I didn't know this life of yours later.

RICHARD: How long ago later?

LOUISE: I haven't seen you in six years.

RICHARD: Oh.

(RICHARD *looks down at his hand. He lets go of* LOUISE's *hand.*)

LOUISE: Can you tell me, was I in any picture?

RICHARD: I don't think so.

LOUISE: Harris told me he showed one. One picture of me.

RICHARD: What were you doing in this picture?

LOUISE: I stood with you. You don't remember that?

RICHARD: Where you stood with me?

LOUISE: Yes.

RICHARD: I'm sorry. What did you look like in this picture?

LOUISE: I was dressed up. You were dressed up too. For a party. For Harris. His parents gave a formal party. When Harris got out of school. And we went to his house, you and I, this huge home.

RICHARD: That was you?

LOUISE: Yes.

RICHARD: That picture. You look better than in the picture.

LOUISE: Well, I haven't seen it.

RICHARD: Your face is more particular. Very particular.

LOUISE: In what way, particular?

RICHARD: I would remember your face. In the picture I did not.

LOUISE: Why, is it out of focus, my face? Washed out?

RICHARD: I don't know. But I remember that picture. I liked it. Yes. I was dressed in a tie. And I wore a hat. I looked very clean. And in this picture I could see a big lawn. And balloons in a tree. A paper lantern. And I was with a pretty woman. In a long dress. I could tell I thought she was pretty. I could see in my eyes how pretty. But she had no particular face. I couldn't make out her face. (Pause) I must have been very stupid. If I behaved dangerously toward you.

LOUISE: How do you know? You can't remember.

RICHARD: I can know it was stupid.

LOUISE: Well, I thought so too.

RICHARD: Good. I guess we agree.

LOUISE: This is a hell of a way to agree.

RICHARD: I agree.

(Pause)

LOUISE: You seem to have the idea, or impression, that I was good to you.

RICHARD: I think that's obvious. It's a good visit. I'm enjoying this visit.

LOUISE: You are, huh?

RICHARD: I can feel it, yes. I'm perking up. Inside.
Getting perky again.

LOUISE: Inside?

RICHARD: Yes, that's where it starts. We know that,
don't we? Harris says that.

LOUISE: Harris said that? Harris came in here and said
the word, perky?

RICHARD: I think so.

LOUISE: I didn't know you talked to Harris.

RICHARD: I didn't. I listened.

LOUISE: Uh huh. But you're talking with me.

RICHARD: You asked about Malcolm Cribbs. I had to
explain Malcolm Cribbs to you.

LOUISE: That's the only reason?

RICHARD: No. You seem good to me.

LOUISE: Okay, but why? What exactly gives you that
impression? If you don't remember.

(Pause)

RICHARD: You think I've been here a long time. Three
months. You think I've lost all judgement?

LOUISE: I don't think that.

RICHARD: You think I'm desperate in here?

LOUISE: I don't think that either.

RICHARD: Why not?

LOUISE: I never thought you were anything but
independent. Completely on your own. The only
person I know who is afraid, I think, if for some reason
you are not alone.

RICHARD: Does that mean I'm not desperate?

LOUISE: I don't know if you're desperate.

(Pause)

RICHARD: Invisible.

LOUISE: What?

RICHARD: I said, Invisible.

LOUISE: What's invisible?

(Pause)

RICHARD: There were woods. Dark woods. Near a
house. Where my parents lived. A forest. I ran into this
forest. Away from a house. I wanted to have adventure.
Excitement. Get lost. And so I did get lost, really lost.
I felt fear. And in this fear I came to a clearing in the
woods. Where I sat down. And closed my eyes. To shut
out all danger. This fear. I wanted nothing to strike,
or hurt me. I wanted to be invisible. Be made invisible.
So nothing would see me in this forest. Nothing in this
world would hurt.
   Or take me away.
   And then I thought, God. He must be invisible. He
can't be seen. And then I thought, I realized, I must be
invisible too. To all danger. In this world. His invisible
child. And then I felt my feet, they relaxed. And in my
knees, my legs, my whole neck, everything in me was
relaxed. And I thought, I must be invisible now. This is
invisible. This is good. I must be safe.
   And so I got up from the ground. I saw everything
around which couldn't hurt me now. There was no
danger. At all in the world. I could see too every step
to take, which way to go. Until I walked right out of
that forest. To a house. I walked through the house into
a room. It was my room. Where I first wanted to run
away and be lost in the woods. And I think that's the
happiest I have ever been. When I lay down on my bed,
the same bed again, and I thanked God who made me

invisible. Made me safe from any danger. So nothing could hurt me. *(Pause. Realizing)* We talked about this. Didn't we talk about this?

LOUISE: Yes. We did. We talked about epiphanies.

RICHARD: Epiphanies?

LOUISE: Or visions. Yes. A long time ago.

RICHARD: What visions?

LOUISE: When we're happy. The happiest. Like an epiphany. When we understand. When life is perfect. It just as well might end.

RICHARD: Perfect.

LOUISE: Uh huh. Because how could it ever get better.

RICHARD: Epiphany.

LOUISE: Yes. I got it from somewhere, that word.

RICHARD: And I told you that? That was my epiphany?

LOUISE: You did.

RICHARD: And you told an epiphany. Your epiphany.

LOUISE: Yes, I did.

RICHARD: It was better than mine. I remember that.

LOUISE: You never said that.

RICHARD: No, mine was being invisible. Yours was better.

LOUISE: Really? What made it better?

RICHARD: I don't know.

LOUISE: Well, there you are.

RICHARD: I know it was better.

LOUISE: I guess I think so too.

RICHARD: See, your epiphany was better.
We're agreeing again.

LOUISE: Uh huh, yes.

RICHARD: Tell it to me again.

LOUISE: Oh, I don't know.

RICHARD: Yes. I want to hear it.

LOUISE: I don't know. What if I'm sad?

RICHARD: Why? I'm not sad.

LOUISE: I know. That's good you're not sad.

RICHARD: It's good for you too.

LOUISE: I'm sure, yes.

RICHARD: So don't be sad.

LOUISE: Okay.

RICHARD: I'm the patient.

LOUISE: You are. I know.

RICHARD: So we can be happy about that.

LOUISE: Okay.

RICHARD: Because I think this visit is working.

LOUISE: Good. I'm glad you think so.

RICHARD: Very clearly. It's working.

LOUISE: Yes. You're so reasonable.

RICHARD: What do you mean, reasonable?

LOUISE: Well, you smile. You nod. You're perky. You're
better at this. A better patient. Much more reasonable.

RICHARD: You're not reasonable?

LOUISE: No. I don't feel like a reasonable visitor. (*Goes to
a window. Pause*) The epiphany I told was when my
father died. When I went home from school. And after

being at home, a few days or so, my mother asked me to go to the attic. To pack some things. *(Pause)* You don't remember this? You don't remember my father died?

RICHARD: No.

LOUISE: There are certain things I'm finding it hard if you can't remember. *(Pause)* This is disconcerting. I didn't realize. I get these disconcerting moments in here. *(Pause)* I'm sorry. You should have heard the speeches in my head. What I remembered, as I drove down. The hindsight. I had such a clear perspective. Because when Harris told me, I thought, I will come. I will come immediately and help this man. I will get him out of here. Get him on with his life. Like I have mine. *(Pause)* When I come back again, in a few days, to visit, I'll tell you that epiphany.

RICHARD: Okay.

LOUISE: But you could help. It would help me. If you thought about it. We can make a bargain, okay? You see what you can remember. Like about my father. And then I'll tell you.

(Pause. RICHARD stands. He slowly walks downstage. He comes to a stop at the other window. He looks out.)

RICHARD: Can you tell me, meantime, if it's a bargain, what you see out there?

LOUISE: Outside?

RICHARD: Yes. I'd like to know what you see outside.

(Pause)

LOUISE: I see that we're on the third floor up. There's a building across from us, to the left. It also has bars. And between these two buildings is a parking lot. And then a lawn. With a couple of trees, oak trees, and a bench. And a person walking, very slowly, pacing by the bench. And beyond are some more buildings. And a road. Not much else. Just some hills. And a lot of sky. *(Pause)* What do you see?

(Pause)

RICHARD: Can you tell me about the room?

LOUISE: What I see in it?

RICHARD: Yes. Tell me about the visiting room.

(Pause)

LOUISE: What I see in this room are four green walls. And two windows. With bars in them, sturdy, like they can never be moved. And over there is a door with bars in it too. And that door is open. And through there I can see part of the dayroom. And beyond that a hallway. The hallway I came down. On my way to visit. *(Pause)* Then there's a clock on the wall. And a picture of a little river, or stream, going through the woods. Four chairs, I think. Ceiling lights. Linoleum. Lots of linoleum squares going straight out, flat, all the way to the next room. *(Pause)* What do you see?

RICHARD: I don't think we see the same room.

LOUISE: No? What room do you see?

RICHARD: It's different.

LOUISE: Tell me. Tell me for example what's different?

RICHARD: I don't see green.

LOUISE: Pale green?

RICHARD: No.

LOUISE: What do you see?

RICHARD: White.

LOUISE: You see white walls?

RICHARD: Yes. And I don't see a picture with a river in the woods.

LOUISE: You don't?

RICHARD: No.

(LOUISE *goes to the picture.*)

LOUISE: It's right here.

RICHARD: That's the picture?

LOUISE: Yes.

RICHARD: Okay.

LOUISE: What did you think it was?

RICHARD: I never saw it.

LOUISE: No? Do you see it now?

RICHARD: Yes.

LOUISE: And what does it look like now?

RICHARD: It looks like a mirror.

LOUISE: A mirror?

RICHARD: Uh huh. That's what I think.

LOUISE: Did you ever look in this mirror?

RICHARD: No, I didn't.

LOUISE: Well, then, why don't you come take a look?

(*Pause*)

RICHARD: Can you bring it to me?

LOUISE: The picture?

RICHARD: Yes.

(LOUISE *takes the picture off the wall and brings it to* RICHARD. *Pause*)

LOUISE: What's it look like now?

RICHARD: It could be a river. A picture of a river.

LOUISE: But you're not sure?

RICHARD: It's a little river.

LOUISE: You thought it was a mirror?

RICHARD: Thank you for telling me.

LOUISE: Yes?

RICHARD: Nobody told me there was a river.

(Pause)

LOUISE: How about the clock?

RICHARD: Hm?

LOUISE: On the other wall. The clock.

RICHARD: I don't see a clock.

LOUISE: No? What's it look like then?

RICHARD: I don't know.

LOUISE: You see nothing up there?

RICHARD: It looks like a plate.

LOUISE: Oh?

RICHARD: Somebody left an empty plate on the wall.

(Pause)

LOUISE: Is there something else? Anything else I should tell you about this room?

RICHARD: The floor.

LOUISE: What about it?

RICHARD: Do you think the floor is straight?

LOUISE: Reasonably straight, yes.

RICHARD: I don't think it's so straight. Feels crooked.
The bars too. The bars don't stay put in the windows
the way you said.

LOUISE: No? What do they do?

RICHARD: I think they advance sometimes. They come
up to my face, they advance on it. Press.

LOUISE: They press on your face?

RICHARD: Yes.

LOUISE: You don't think you do that?

RICHARD: What do I do?

LOUISE: You don't think you walk up to them. Like just
now, the windows. You walked up to the window.

RICHARD: I'm sure I walk up to the window.

LOUISE: Then that's the advancing.

RICHARD: No. They advance faster than I walk.

LOUISE: You sure of that?

RICHARD: Than I advance, yes.

LOUISE: How do you know that?

RICHARD: I just see it.

LOUISE: You should tell me.

RICHARD: I'm trying to tell.

LOUISE: Then tell it again.

(Pause)

RICHARD: It's better today. There's hardly any
advancing.

(LOUISE *puts the painting back on the wall.*)

LOUISE: How about outside?

RICHARD: It's too bright outside.

LOUISE: You can't see out there?

RICHARD: No.

(Pause)

LOUISE: How about me? Can you see me?

RICHARD: It's okay.

LOUISE: No, is my face washed out? Like a plate?

RICHARD: A little. Yes.

(Pause)

LOUISE: *(Nervously)* They told me up front. They told me this, the nurses. That you can barely make it to bed. Or to meals. And probably from now on when you walk, you can never be sure if you're moving, or if it's the room. *(Pause)* The thing I don't understand is how you manage to slug somebody called Malcolm Cribbs in the middle of all this.

RICHARD: Malcolm Cribbs makes me focus.

LOUISE: He does?

RICHARD: Yes. He stops it moving. He stops the room.

LOUISE: How?

RICHARD: Because I want to hit him. I want to point out something else.

LOUISE: What's that?

RICHARD: I made it to the window.

LOUISE: Yes, you did.

RICHARD: Nobody helped. Even Malcolm Cribbs.

LOUISE: I'm glad.

RICHARD: You want to help me back?

LOUISE: Yes, I do.

RICHARD: Okay. I want to go back to the chair.

(LOUISE *goes to* RICHARD. *She leads him back to the chair. They sit down.)*

RICHARD: *(Pleasantly)* Do you like to sit with a person who can't see the same room?

LOUISE: It's okay.

RICHARD: Do you think we should see the same room?

LOUISE: Yes. I think we should.

(Pause)

RICHARD: You said you live somewhere. You live in a better place.

LOUISE: I live in a house.

RICHARD: Where is it? Your house?

LOUISE: It's north of here. About four hours.

RICHARD: Uh huh. You like it?

LOUISE: Yes. I like to come back to it. I travel.

RICHARD: Travel?

LOUISE: I travel, yes, quite a bit. I have to go places.

RICHARD: What places?

LOUISE: Well, to sing.

RICHARD: You sing?

LOUISE: Uh huh. That's what I do.

RICHARD: I didn't know that.

LOUISE: Well, I do that. I write songs. Lots of songs, and I travel. Go to clubs in Pennsylvania. Little cafes in New York, or Vermont. Lots of states. Lots of places in a beat-up car that worries me. I go to festivals too, where I open for other people, much better known singers. I sing before these people come on. And sometimes these people, they want to sing too what I write. Which is what I want. Because then I won't have to go all over, like now. Because I like to travel, I do, but deep down I like my home better. I like the land where I live. I have some woods and a field, and I feel I could stay still there. Stay at home. And just write. Try to write songs. These other songs. Which I hope to write.

(Pause)

RICHARD: What kind of songs?

LOUISE: Well, a mixture. Mainly folk songs.

RICHARD: Folk songs, uh huh.

LOUISE: Yes.

RICHARD: You like that, then? Folk songs?

LOUISE: Yes. I like the things I can say.

RICHARD: What things?

LOUISE: Well, things that sound better, probably, with a little music.

RICHARD: Can you tell me?

LOUISE: Tell you?

RICHARD: Something from a folk song.

LOUISE: No, I don't think so.

RICHARD: Give me some words.

LOUISE: What words?

RICHARD: Words you sing.

LOUISE: No, I don't know.

RICHARD: Please. I want to listen.

LOUISE: No, it would be very hard, I think, to sing in here.

RICHARD: Just say them.

LOUISE: I'll say them another time.

RICHARD: Write them down.

LOUISE: What?

RICHARD: Write some words down that you sing.
So I can keep them.

LOUISE: Okay. Okay, I'll write some words down. I will.
When I leave.

RICHARD: When you leave?

LOUISE: Yes. I'll leave you with some words. Something
I sing.

RICHARD: Okay.

LOUISE: I promise. Just remind me. To write some
words.

RICHARD: Uh huh. Did you used to sing when we knew
each other?

LOUISE: Well, yes. I sang protest songs.

RICHARD: Yes?

LOUISE: Yes. That kind of song.

RICHARD: You seem embarrassed.

LOUISE: I'm not embarrassed.

RICHARD: No?

LOUISE: Well, no. It's what we sang then, that's all.
Nothing too deep, or poetic. Literally minded protest
songs. And you used to sing along too. Or hum,
or something.

RICHARD: I can sing too?

LOUISE: No, I didn't say that.

RICHARD: I can't sing?

LOUISE: Well, I don't know if you can sing. You didn't sing.

RICHARD: Hmm.

LOUISE: It's okay. Lots of people can't particularly sing. It's not a big deal. Not at all. *(Pause)* Why are you looking at me like that?

RICHARD: What?

LOUISE: You seem to be looking.

RICHARD: I'm trying to remember if you sing.

LOUISE: If I sing, okay, I see.

RICHARD: I'm trying to do that.

LOUISE: No, of course.

RICHARD: Is there something wrong?

LOUISE: No, nothing wrong.

RICHARD: Okay.

LOUISE: Why don't you try remembering my father?

RICHARD: What?

LOUISE: My father, remember? You're supposed to try to remember my father. Before he died.

RICHARD: Did I like your father?

LOUISE: No. Not particularly.

RICHARD: Then why should I remember him?

LOUISE: Because you agreed. That's our bargain. And because he's probably a little like Malcolm Cribbs. He might focus you. Get you going.

RICHARD: Did I used to hit your father?

LOUISE: No, but you argued. You were very clear when you argued. I remember. I was impressed.

RICHARD: With what I argued?

LOUISE: Yes.

RICHARD: I don't remember. I don't remember your father.

(Pause)

LOUISE: You came home with me. To their house. And we sat down. We sat down to dinner, you and I, with my parents. And my father said the blessing. And then he paused, and added, that it was a shame. This thing in Indochina was a shame. Like it was still a part of the blessing. And I thought for a moment. I thought, I respect this man. I have accepted his viewpoint since I can remember. He is moral. And strict. He has taught me to be honest, taught me discipline. He has also frightened me. And I hope his intention isn't to embarrass.

   But then I heard you. I heard you quietly ask, What shame, sir, exactly, do you have in mind? And so my father said, It's a shame, don't you think, if the other peoples in this world have begun to perceive us as weak. That is, if we cannot stand by the commitments we have made. And then you said, No. Perhaps not. Perhaps they perceive us as finally coming to our senses. So my father asked, What senses, could you mean? And you told my father there was a confusion involved here. A false assumption, if we confuse our religious beliefs with the imposition of a secular viewpoint, or setup, that may be inappropriate to the rest of the world. And further, you said, Our secular viewpoint may indeed be limiting, or a diminution, of what God had originally in mind.

(Pause)

RICHARD: I said that?

LOUISE: Yes, you did.

RICHARD: Those words? All of them?

LOUISE: Well, it sounded okay.

RICHARD: I don't talk like that with Malcolm Cribbs.

LOUISE: No, I know. You hit him.

RICHARD: Then what did he answer?

LOUISE: My father?

RICHARD: I want to know.

LOUISE: I don't remember.

RICHARD: Really?

LOUISE: No. I was listening to you. *(Pause)* Why are you looking like that?

RICHARD: I'm trying to remember your father.

LOUISE: But you're looking at my mouth. Is there something wrong with my mouth?

RICHARD: No, nothing is wrong.

LOUISE: Then why are you so focused on my mouth?

RICHARD: I didn't know I was focused.

LOUISE: I'm sorry.

RICHARD: I didn't mean to focus.

LOUISE: No, I'm sorry. You just seem stuck a little.

RICHARD: I was stuck on your mouth?

LOUISE: Well, no, it's not the first time, Richard. You go blank sometimes. And then you stare. You stare at these parts of me.

RICHARD: What parts?

LOUISE: Well, my forehead. My knee. My breast. You've stared at my breast.

RICHARD: I'm sorry.

LOUISE: No, I'm sure you have to do that. I know you have to do that.

RICHARD: Maybe I have to remember each thing first.

LOUISE: Well, I suppose so.

RICHARD: Maybe if I remember one thing, then maybe I'll remember the whole impression.

LOUISE: I'm sorry I mentioned it.

RICHARD: No, I understand.

LOUISE: No, it's not reasonable to pick at you like that.

RICHARD: It is reasonable. I think it's reasonable. We are trying to get along. You should tell me if I bother you. We should begin with that.

LOUISE: Okay.

RICHARD: Being polite is not going to help me. How can I remember you, what bothers you, if you're polite?

LOUISE: You're right.

RICHARD: So you should tell me. Anything that bothers you.

(Pause)

LOUISE: Okay, Richard. It unnerves me when you choose one part of my body and you stare at it.

RICHARD: I'll try to control it better.

LOUISE: Okay. Because you make me feel like an apparition.

RICHARD: I'll calm down on the staring.

LOUISE: Yes. And I'll try not to notice it so much.

RICHARD: You'll let me stare?

LOUISE: Well, some.

RICHARD: Okay.

LOUISE: We'll just keep discussing it, okay?

RICHARD: Okay.

(Pause)

LOUISE: Richard, come on.

RICHARD: What?

LOUISE: You should still look. There's nothing wrong with looking.

RICHARD: No, I think I should look at some other things too.

LOUISE: Richard.

RICHARD: No, there are other things I should be looking at in here.

LOUISE: Like what?

RICHARD: What if there's another picture in here? Another river or something.

LOUISE: There's no other picture.

RICHARD: Okay. That's good.

LOUISE: Only one picture. One clock. So don't worry.

RICHARD: Don't worry either if I look at you.

LOUISE: I'm not worried.

RICHARD: Because I'll look again when I'm ready to look.

LOUISE: Well, I'm ready.

RICHARD: Okay.

LOUISE: Whenever you're ready. *(She steps across the room. She looks at the picture on the wall.)* I had forgotten how intently you can look at something. Which is funny. Because that's what was most particular about you. How intently you could look. I just think you do it

more. It's a little more now. *(Playfully)* It's reached the
level of a stare. *(Pause)* I remember the first time coming
down a flight of stairs. And in the bottom hallway
you were standing over by a wall. Many people were
milling around, students, but you seemed separate.
Very silent. You seemed to be looking intently at some
spot in the hall. I couldn't see what spot. And I didn't
know you at all, but I found myself stepping up to you,
into this spot, something compelled me to speak. And
I think the first thing I ever said to you was, You don't
look real. Sometimes when I've seen you, you don't
look real. *(Pause)* That's what I said. That's a funny
way to begin, don't you think? For a man and a woman
to begin? With a statement like that? *(Pause)* Richard?

*(LOUISE goes to RICHARD. She sits. She reaches forward and
takes his hand.)*

LOUISE: Richard? What's going on?

(Pause)

RICHARD: *(Flatly)* I can't feel your hand.

LOUISE: You can't feel it?

RICHARD: No.

LOUISE: I'm holding your hand, but you can't feel it?

RICHARD: No, I can't. *(Watches the room)*

LOUISE: What about before?

RICHARD: I don't know.

LOUISE: When I held your hand before.

RICHARD: A little bit.

LOUISE: You felt it a little bit?

RICHARD: Yes.

LOUISE: Does it make a difference if I squeeze it?

RICHARD: No.

LOUISE: No difference?

RICHARD: No.

LOUISE: How about your other hand?

RICHARD: I can't feel it.

LOUISE: Same thing with this other hand?

RICHARD: Yes.

(Pause)

LOUISE: Let's hold it anyway.

(RICHARD *continues to watch the room.*)

LOUISE: Does this happen a lot?

RICHARD: I think so.

LOUISE: When?

RICHARD: A lot.

LOUISE: Does it frighten you?

RICHARD: Yes.

LOUISE: What should I do? When you're frightened?

RICHARD: You should stay.

LOUISE: Is that going to help? If I sit here?

RICHARD: Yes. *(Pause)* It's getting extra white in here.

LOUISE: What is?

RICHARD: The walls are white.

LOUISE: Extra white?

RICHARD: Yes. *(Pause)* You're going to have to tell me your name again. I'm forgetting your name.

LOUISE: Louise.

RICHARD: Thank you. Louise.

LOUISE: Do you want me to write it down?

RICHARD: What?

LOUISE: My name. You won't have to remember my name. I'll write it down.

(LOUISE *reaches for her shoulder bag. She takes out a pencil and piece of paper with one hand. She writes her name. She hands it to* RICHARD.)

LOUISE: Here it is. My name.

RICHARD: This is your name?

LOUISE: Yes. Louise.

RICHARD: Louise.

LOUISE: That's right. You can hold onto my name.

RICHARD: Thank you, Louise.

LOUISE: Wherever you go. You can have my name.

RICHARD: Okay.

LOUISE: They can send you back to me.

RICHARD: Okay.

(*Pause*)

LOUISE: Richard, you seem better. Are you better?

(*Pause*)

RICHARD: Is anybody coming?

LOUISE: From where?

RICHARD: In the other room.

LOUISE: No.

RICHARD: There's a man called Malcolm Cribbs. He should be coming.

LOUISE: Why's that?

RICHARD: He can tell.

LOUISE: What does he tell?

RICHARD: He knows when the room gets like this.

LOUISE: Gets white?

RICHARD: That's why he comes.

LOUISE: I see. How does he know when to come?

RICHARD: I don't know.

LOUISE: But you hit him?

RICHARD: Yes. I have to hit him.

LOUISE: Richard, don't get up.

RICHARD: Malcolm Cribbs is coming. It's better if I get up.

LOUISE: *(Restraining him)* No. No, there's nobody coming.

RICHARD: Nobody from out there?

LOUISE: Nobody.

(Pause)

RICHARD: Maybe he's not coming.

LOUISE: He isn't. No.

RICHARD: Maybe he knows you're here. That's why he's not coming.

LOUISE: Maybe, yes.

(RICHARD *looks at the piece of paper in his hand.)*

RICHARD: Louise.

LOUISE: That's right. Louise.

(Pause)

RICHARD: Can we take a walk, Louise?

LOUISE: Where would you like?

RICHARD: Around the room.

LOUISE: Okay.

RICHARD: I need to walk.

LOUISE: I understand.

RICHARD: I don't want to forget again.

LOUISE: Come on then.

RICHARD: I don't want to start up again.

LOUISE: Come on. Let's get up.

(LOUISE *helps* RICHARD *out of the chair.*)

LOUISE: You ready?

RICHARD: Yes.

LOUISE: Where do you want to go?

RICHARD: Around the room.

LOUISE: This direction?

RICHARD: That's good.

LOUISE: How about the river?

RICHARD: What river?

LOUISE: You want to walk down to the river?
The one in the woods?

RICHARD: Okay.

LOUISE: Good. Let's take a walk to the river.

RICHARD: Okay.

(LOUISE *leads* RICHARD *slowly toward the picture on the wall.*)

LOUISE: How are we doing?

RICHARD: I'm feeling better.

LOUISE: We're almost there.

RICHARD: We're almost at the river?

LOUISE: Yes, it's a good river. I've seen it.

RICHARD: Where?

LOUISE: Just ahead. See that bright spot?

RICHARD: Okay.

LOUISE: Just a little more ahead.

RICHARD: Thank you.

LOUISE: For what?

RICHARD: Getting out of that chair.

LOUISE: You're welcome.

RICHARD: It's not always so good in that chair.

LOUISE: No, I know. I could see.

(They stop in front of the picture.)

RICHARD: This is it?

LOUISE: Yes. The river. We're at the river.

RICHARD: *(Peering forward)* Pretty small for a river.

LOUISE: Well, it's more a stream.

RICHARD: Looks nice.

LOUISE: I think so too. I'm glad to be here.

RICHARD: Can we sit down?

LOUISE: By the river?

RICHARD: Yes. I want to sit down.

LOUISE: Is this good right here? You're all right for sitting?

RICHARD: It's good.

LOUISE: Good. Let's sit down.

(They sit down in two chairs underneath the picture of the stream.)

LOUISE: How do you like it?

RICHARD: It's nice.

LOUISE: We should come here more often.

RICHARD: Okay.

LOUISE: Things look different.

RICHARD: Yes.

LOUISE: How's your hand?

RICHARD: It's okay.

LOUISE: Can you feel anything?

RICHARD: I can feel it.

LOUISE: A little bit, yes?

RICHARD: Yes.

LOUISE: Good. I'm glad it's back.

RICHARD: I got to rest.

LOUISE: Excuse me?

RICHARD: I have to rest my head.

LOUISE: Yes, okay. Rest your head.

(RICHARD leans forward. He rests his head on LOUISE's shoulder. He closes his eyes. He sleeps.)

(CARLA appears at the door.)

CARLA: You moved him.

LOUISE: Yes. We moved.

CARLA: He looks better over there.

LOUISE: Thank you.

CARLA: He's not leaning so straight up.

LOUISE: That's right.

CARLA: Must be relaxing. *(She steps into the room. She takes a chair. She sits.)* I took a nap too.

LOUISE: Yes?

CARLA: A very deep nap.

LOUISE: That's nice.

CARLA: In this nap I saw soldiers. Soldiers again making incursions.

LOUISE: Oh, yes?

CARLA: Coming up the mountainside, yeah, many foot soldiers. Chasing and shouting. They looted and burned. And in this nap I escaped up a stream, I climbed up many ledges. I held my rifle to kill the first man who dared to capture me.

LOUISE: Uh huh.

CARLA: Quite a nap.

LOUISE: Yes, I think so.

CARLA: But in this nap, later, I met somebody else who is using my feet.

LOUISE: Did you, really?

CARLA: Finally, yeah. What a relief.

LOUISE: Who was it?

CARLA: Looked like a young lady. Pretty. Very innocent. Like a girl.

LOUISE: That's good.

CARLA: An exuberant girl. Yeah. With balls of fire in her eyes. And I was all alone, standing on a little ledge, waiting for soldiers. And she came to me, from nowhere, and asked. She said, Can I have your feet? I need your feet. I cannot find where mine are gone.

LOUISE: And what did you say?

CARLA: I said, Sure. I won't be needing these.

LOUISE: You said that?

CARLA: Yeah, I was very generous. In this nap.

LOUISE: But why yours?

CARLA: Hm?

LOUISE: Why did she want your particular feet?

CARLA: I didn't find out.

LOUISE: You didn't ask?

CARLA: I said I was busy.

LOUISE: You were what?

CARLA: Busy, yeah. I had to wake up.

LOUISE: What for? You should have talked to her.

CARLA: I'm going to talk. Later.

LOUISE: You had her right there. In your nap.

CARLA: I made an appointment.

LOUISE: What?

CARLA: Uh huh. To talk.

LOUISE: But what if she doesn't come back?

CARLA: She's coming back.

LOUISE: No. She might not.

CARLA: We're going to talk. At the appointment.

LOUISE: No, they don't keep appointments. You cannot make an appointment like that. To keep in your sleep.

CARLA: *(With quiet assurance)* She's keeping it. She told me.

(Pause)

LOUISE: Well, okay. I believe you.

CARLA: I believe it too. I can feel it. I can feel it in my feet. She's coming back to me.

(Blackout)

END OF ACT ONE

ACT TWO

(The same. Two weeks later. RICHARD *sits in a chair. A soccer ball is on the floor by the wall.* LOUISE *enters with a shoulder bag. She stands at the door.)*

LOUISE: Hello.

(Pause)

LOUISE: Hello, Richard.

RICHARD: Louise.

LOUISE: Yes.

RICHARD: Hi. Louise Wick.

(Pause)

LOUISE: You look different. You're different today.

RICHARD: Thank you.

LOUISE: What's different?

RICHARD: I don't know.

(Pause)

LOUISE: Is it your shirt?

RICHARD: Hm?

LOUISE: You're wearing a new shirt.

RICHARD: I don't think it's a shirt.

LOUISE: Then are you perky maybe? Last time you said you felt perky. Just a little bit.

RICHARD: I don't know if it's perky.

LOUISE: Well, I don't either. It's something.

RICHARD: I could be perky.

LOUISE: Look at me.

(They look at each other across the room.)

LOUISE: I can't tell what's different.

RICHARD: I was hoping to see you.

LOUISE: What, last week?

RICHARD: You had jobs. They told me.

LOUISE: Yes, that's right. I went off to Toronto.

RICHARD: You sang in Toronto?

LOUISE: Yep.

RICHARD: Did it go well in Toronto?

LOUISE: Yes. It went well. *(Pause)* You look like you can see me. Is that what's different?

RICHARD: I can see.

LOUISE: You can see all the way over here? I don't look washed out?

RICHARD: You look nice.

(Pause)

LOUISE: Well, that's different. If you can see me. That's a big difference. *(Comes into the room. She sits. She puts aside her shoulder bag.)*

RICHARD: I've been practicing.

LOUISE: You've practiced what?

RICHARD: Just looking, that's all. In the distance.

LOUISE: Okay.

RICHARD: Uh huh. Some other things too.

LOUISE: Like what?

RICHARD: I've taken a couple of walks.

LOUISE: In here?

RICHARD: Uh huh. Lots of walks in here.

LOUISE: Where'd you go?

RICHARD: Well, to the river.

LOUISE: Uh huh.

RICHARD: Several times. To the river.

LOUISE: You like that walk?

RICHARD: Yes, I do. You want to see me stand?

LOUISE: Okay.

(RICHARD *stands. He takes a couple of steps.*)

RICHARD: It's not moving.

LOUISE: What?

RICHARD: Nothing moves. In this room. Just me.

LOUISE: Oh. That's a big change, isn't it? If nothing moves.

RICHARD: I hope so. (*Turns back to the chair. He sits.*) I've been to the window too.

LOUISE: Good.

RICHARD: A couple of times, yeah. I'd like to go out sometime.

LOUISE: What did you see at the window?

RICHARD: What did I see?

LOUISE: Yes.

RICHARD: I saw a bench.

LOUISE: Uh huh.

RICHARD: You don't remember the bench?

LOUISE: No. I guess, I don't. (*Stands. She goes downstage to a window.*)

LOUISE: Yes. There's a bench.

RICHARD: Uh huh. I saw it.

LOUISE: What else did you see?

RICHARD: I was interested in the bench.

LOUISE: Just the bench?

RICHARD: I didn't want to look down. I wanted to keep my eyes on the bench.

LOUISE: Look down at what?

RICHARD: I think we should go sit on it. I would like to do that.

LOUISE: Okay.

RICHARD: We can do that? Go down out there and sit on that bench?

LOUISE: Well, we could. Nobody's on it. It's empty.

RICHARD: Uh huh. Someday then, okay? When they let me outside.

LOUISE: Okay. We'll sit on it.

RICHARD: It's a date?

LOUISE: A date? Yes, a date.

RICHARD: Good. We have a date.

(LOUISE *steps away from the window.*)

LOUISE: What's that? By your chair.

(RICHARD *looks down. He picks up the soccer ball.*)

RICHARD: I've been practicing this too.

LOUISE: Yes?

RICHARD: Harris gave me this. Before.

LOUISE: They let you kick that in here?

RICHARD: I'm just holding it. *(Pause)* Last night, in the middle of the night, I woke up. I remembered a lawn. Or a field. I think it was you. You used to stand over there, I think. Where you are now. And I would stand here. About this distance. And I had a ball. Which I would push with my feet. And you pushed it back. We would kick passes. We ran down the field together. Kicking passes. That's what I remember. Before Harris. Before many things. I remember practicing with a soccer ball.

(Pause)

LOUISE: Can I see it?

RICHARD: Yes.

(LOUISE goes to RICHARD. She takes the soccer ball.)

RICHARD: Last night I realized how I used to keep this ball in the air. How I used to bounce it on my foot. I would do this, on each foot. And bounce it on my knees. Or on my head. My shoulders. I could bounce this ball everywhere on my body. For hours. I used to practice over and over again. Like this ball was my own room. I could go to this ball and be in my own private room. *(Pause)* I used to show off to you?

LOUISE: Yes, you did.

RICHARD: I thought so.

LOUISE: You used to bounce it all over.

(Pause)

RICHARD: I can hardly throw this ball up now. And catch it.

(LOUISE hands the soccer ball back.)

LOUISE: Do it now.

RICHARD: What?

LOUISE: Throw it. I want you to throw the ball to me.

(RICHARD *stands. He tosses the ball.* LOUISE *catches it.*)

LOUISE: You catch it.

RICHARD: I'm going to catch?

LOUISE: Yes, you are.

RICHARD: Okay.

(LOUISE *tosses the ball. It bounces off* RICHARD'*s chest and away from him.* LOUISE *retrieves it.*)

LOUISE: I'm going to do it from closer.

RICHARD: Okay.

LOUISE: This should work if we're closer.

(LOUISE *gently tosses the ball.* RICHARD *catches it in his arms.*)

LOUISE: Now give it back.

RICHARD: I want to rest.

LOUISE: No, Richard. Throw it back.

RICHARD: I have to sit down.

LOUISE: No. I want you to throw the ball.

(RICHARD *throws the ball.* LOUISE *catches it. She tosses it back. He catches it.*)

LOUISE: Okay. Sit down.

(RICHARD *sits down.*)

RICHARD: This ball used to go very slow. When I kicked it, it used to stay in the air for me. I had all this time when it stayed in the air. *(Pause)* It's not like that now. It speeded up.

LOUISE: It'll get slower. I'm sure. You'll make it go slow again. You will. Two weeks ago you didn't even remember. You had no idea. It's much better now. How you look, Richard. You're more alert. You sit up so much more relaxed now.

(Pause. RICHARD smiles.)

RICHARD: My eyes.

LOUISE: What?

RICHARD: I said, My eyes.

LOUISE: What about them?

RICHARD: Is there anything new in my eyes?

LOUISE: New?

RICHARD: Uh huh. Different. Something you never saw before.

(Pause)

LOUISE: You're not staring. I haven't seen you get stuck. In a stare.

RICHARD: You didn't catch me?

LOUISE: Staring, no. Not so far.

RICHARD: Good.

LOUISE: No, I haven't.

RICHARD: I don't want my eyes to stare at you. Like last time.

LOUISE: Well, Richard, it wasn't all the time.

RICHARD: Sometimes.

LOUISE: Yes, it was, sometimes.

RICHARD: I want to look casually at you.

LOUISE: Well, you are. You're looking casual.

RICHARD: I've been practicing that.

LOUISE: Good for you.

RICHARD: Because I want to go out in public with you.

LOUISE: Okay.

RICHARD: Public, yes. After we sit on the bench, we can go shopping. Or out to a restaurant. Because I can look casually again.

LOUISE: Yes, you can. You're not so pent up.

RICHARD: Pent up. That's right. I'm perky now.

LOUISE: Right. Exactly.

RICHARD: I was perky last time too. But this is better.

LOUISE: It's deeper.

RICHARD: Deeper perky.

LOUISE: Right. You could probably even glance now.

RICHARD: Glance?

LOUISE: Casually glance, yes. With your eyes.

RICHARD: Yes, I can. I have a casual glance. I can take a glance now. Like everybody.

LOUISE: Okay.

RICHARD: Because how can I glance, for example, at your breast, if I stare? I mean, what kind of person could do that? Get stuck in a stare in public like that? *(Pause)* You're laughing?

LOUISE: What?

RICHARD: I heard you laugh.

LOUISE: I'm sorry.

RICHARD: You look embarrassed.

LOUISE: I'm not embarrassed.

RICHARD: I'm just explaining.

LOUISE: No, it shouldn't embarrass.

RICHARD: I was explaining and I mentioned about your breast.

LOUISE: That's fine.

RICHARD: I'm sorry.

LOUISE: No, it's fine what you said.

RICHARD: I didn't mean I wanted to see it naked.

LOUISE: No, I know.

RICHARD: I'm not trying to talk about that now.
Or talk later.

LOUISE: I understand.

RICHARD: No, I was bothered you caught me staring,
on your first visit, and that's one thing I decided. That
I was not going to get caught like that again. Staring.
(Pause) When you left, after you did that, I woke up.
I saw you were gone. I decided to go back. To the chair
where I sit alone. So I got up. Started walking. But then
I saw the floor move. I saw the windows advance.
I saw every wall was white. And then I knew my body.
How it could disappear. And the room curl up. Or fold.
(Pause) Except I heard something. Or thought. I could
feel something. A hand. I felt a hand. And in the hand
I looked down and saw a piece of paper. On the paper
I saw your name. I read your name.
   And then I saw the room. It came back. I saw the
chair. I went to it. I sat down. *(Pause)* That was my first
walk. Alone to a chair.

(Pause)

LOUISE: Richard, I'm not embarrassed. It shouldn't
embarrass.

RICHARD: Okay.

LOUISE: I get surprised, that's all. Nervous.

RICHARD: If I stare?

LOUISE: No. You frighten me. It frightens sometimes.

RICHARD: What frightens?

LOUISE: Just some of these feelings.

RICHARD: Can you tell me?

LOUISE: Why? What do you want to know?

RICHARD: If you can tell me.

(Pause)

LOUISE: I'm a little confused right now. Maybe I should go.

RICHARD: What for?

LOUISE: It's enough for now, don't you think?

RICHARD: No, I don't think.

LOUISE: No, I'm sorry, I don't feel presentable, or something, any longer. It feels so abrupt in here. It gets abrupt.

RICHARD: What do you mean, presentable?

LOUISE: Please. Would you let me think?

RICHARD: What?

LOUISE: I need to sit still here a minute. I want to sit by myself, here by the river, and think.

(LOUISE sits in a chair across the room. RICHARD watches.)

RICHARD: I'm thinking too. I'm trying to remember, all week, why I was dangerous.

(No response)

RICHARD: Your father also. Your father at the table when we talked. *(Pause)* I can remember nothing when

I was dangerous. *(Pause)* I remember a house.
I slammed, I think, against a house. And on the
other side of this house, I remember walking up a hill.
To the top. And down below I could see mist. With
trees, a whole woods, and the sound of water. And I
couldn't see my body. It must have been invisible. And
I thought, this is good, this is excellent, it must be early
morning now. I have time now to go where I am going.

    And then I stopped. I stopped halfway up. And I said,
Where am I? What country is this?

    And then I woke up. In a hospital. A hospital before
this one. *(Pause)* I never made it to the top of the hill.

(Pause)

LOUISE: There wasn't any hill. To walk up.

RICHARD: What?

LOUISE: There wasn't a hill. You were on a motorcycle.

RICHARD: What motorcycle?

LOUISE: I don't know. I wasn't there.

RICHARD: Harris told you?

LOUISE: Yes.

(Pause)

RICHARD: Is that why I was dangerous? Motorcycles?

LOUISE: I think there are other things, really, I'd rather
you remember first.

RICHARD: What would you like me to remember first?

LOUISE: Well, that's not up to me, is it?

RICHARD: No?

LOUISE: You're the one who's supposed to remember.

RICHARD: But you should try different things. Even
angry things.

LOUISE: Who said I was angry?

RICHARD: I don't know. I thought maybe.

LOUISE: Is that what you'd like? Something angry?

RICHARD: I want to be angry?

LOUISE: Something angry to remember, yes. Would that get you going again? You could come out slugging?

RICHARD: I'm just asking.

LOUISE: Asking what?

RICHARD: I don't know. Maybe if we used to argue.

LOUISE: No. We did not argue.

RICHARD: Why not?

LOUISE: Because you had nothing to say.

RICHARD: Yeah? I bet I would say now.

LOUISE: No, you wouldn't. Not if you got mad.

RICHARD: No, I would argue now. I would have things to say.

LOUISE: What things?

RICHARD: How should I know? Maybe if I got mad.

LOUISE: No, you'd just get in a mood.

RICHARD: What mood?

LOUISE: Listen, I don't want to argue.

RICHARD: Come on. You can tell me what mood.

LOUISE: No, you'll just make me mad.

RICHARD: Okay, go ahead. I'm listening.

LOUISE: What?

RICHARD: Tell me. Go on, tell me. All the things I used to do. Everything that could make you mad.

LOUISE: But I'm not mad about them now.

RICHARD: Why not?

LOUISE: Because the argument's over. We outgrew it.

RICHARD: I didn't outgrow.

LOUISE: Well, I'm sorry.

RICHARD: I can't even remember. How can I outgrow?

LOUISE: Well, you'll just have to outgrow over there. By yourself. Argue over there with yourself.

RICHARD: You don't want to join in?

LOUISE: No, I'm fine over here.

RICHARD: Come on. Get mad again. Good and mad.

LOUISE: What, is this funny to you?

RICHARD: Please. Tell me about my moods.

LOUISE: What?

RICHARD: My moods. Did they change? Could that make you mad?

LOUISE: Sure, they changed. Like the weather.

RICHARD: *(Proudly)* I thought so.

LOUISE: You're such a fool.

RICHARD: Yeah? And what about your moods?

LOUISE: What?

RICHARD: Did we argue about your moods? Or what a fool you are.

LOUISE: I'm a fool?

RICHARD: Probably, yes, if we argued.

LOUISE: What makes me a fool?

RICHARD: I don't know, you look like you could be a fool.

LOUISE: What is this, a new kind of perky with you?

RICHARD: I'm not perky. I'm asking questions.

LOUISE: We did not argue. I told you.

RICHARD: I don't know. I just have your word for this.

LOUISE: Well, what's your word?

RICHARD: I don't have a word.

LOUISE: Exactly.

RICHARD: Maybe your word is no good either.

LOUISE: It's a word at least.

RICHARD: Could be all wrong, your word. Could be you didn't outgrow either.

LOUISE: Don't look so smug.

RICHARD: No, I think it's good if we argue now.

LOUISE: I'm not arguing.

RICHARD: That's because you don't know any time you're angry.

LOUISE: You don't know yourself.

RICHARD: Yep. I think always there was an argument in here.

LOUISE: What argument?

RICHARD: You look dangerous too.

LOUISE: Me?

RICHARD: Sure. You left me.

LOUISE: What?

RICHARD: You probably should have stayed, I bet.

LOUISE: What for?

RICHARD: Because you could have been exuberant.

LOUISE: What? I needed you to be exuberant?

RICHARD: Yes, you told me.

LOUISE: I never told you. I never said that. We never talked about that.

RICHARD: Nope. I think so.

LOUISE: I was exuberant to begin with.

RICHARD: Nope. I think I made you more.

LOUISE: I did not need you to be exuberant.

RICHARD: No. I remember.

LOUISE: You remember what?

RICHARD: You should have stayed.

LOUISE: Stayed for what?

RICHARD: We could still do that. Be exuberant together.

LOUISE: Oh, yes? Yes? And what would I do now? How would I be doing any of the things I do now?

RICHARD: You could sing.

LOUISE: No, I would not. I would not be singing.

RICHARD: Why not?

LOUISE: Because I was compelled.

RICHARD: What?

LOUISE: It was compelling. To be with you.

RICHARD: I didn't compel.

LOUISE: No, I know. I left.

RICHARD: You're shouting.

LOUISE: What?

RICHARD: You don't have to shout at me you left.

LOUISE: I didn't shout.

RICHARD: Over here you shouted.

LOUISE: No, I did not. I only enunciated, very clearly, that I left.

RICHARD: I heard you left. I want to know what for. I want to know what was dangerous.

LOUISE: You're shouting yourself.

RICHARD: No, just tell me your answer.

LOUISE: What? I'm supposed to answer now for you?

RICHARD: Because you don't have an answer.

LOUISE: What, for you?

RICHARD: Then answer then only for yourself.

LOUISE: I did. I have answered. All by myself. I have answered for six years. And so now you answer. You answer for yourself. *(Pause)* You're staring again.

RICHARD: I'm not staring.

LOUISE: No, you're staring. You're staring, bang, at my mouth.

RICHARD: I'm waiting for some answer.

LOUISE: Well, then, don't stare.

RICHARD: I'm not staring.

LOUISE: How do you expect to get an answer? If you stare?

(Pause)

RICHARD: I think it's unfair to say that. You know what I feel about staring.

(Pause)

LOUISE: I'm sorry I mentioned it. Your stare.

(Pause)

RICHARD: I'm asking to know what made you think I was dangerous.

(Pause)

LOUISE: Because I used to fear for you.

RICHARD: What did you fear?

LOUISE: Something like this. This place.

RICHARD: I could come here?

LOUISE: Yes. I thought so. *(Pause)* And that would be disturbing. Very. If you didn't want to be around. Stay alive. Past a certain point. If you could just slip away some place like this, or any place, just disappear, I would slip too.
   I thought that was dangerous.

(LOUISE takes a chair. She sits beside RICHARD.)

LOUISE: I'm not here, Richard. To argue. *(Pause)* Last night while you were up, in bed, probably I was up. In fact, for two nights I've been up. Ever since I got back from Toronto. Because probably I knew I had to come back. And so I did a little reading. I was restless. I kept thinking, I thought, I seem to have this basic thing in me. That my life began, all my writing, my songs, when I was eighteen. And so I read some of the books I used to read. I looked at Keats. Took a look at Forster. Kazantzakis and Dostoevski. I wanted to read again some of those celebratory perspectives. I wanted to see what made me think life was so abundant. What made me feel like I was born. *(Pause)* Do you remember those people?

RICHARD: No.

LOUISE: Not at all?

RICHARD: I don't think so.

LOUISE: Maybe you should look at them again. Maybe sometime, okay? You could tell me what you think.

RICHARD: What did you think?

(Pause)

LOUISE: When I looked again?

RICHARD: Yes.

LOUISE: I was disappointed. *(Pause)* They seemed overblown. The ideas in there. Distant. They didn't seem enough, I think.
They made me sad.

RICHARD: Sad?

LOUISE: Yes. That they weren't enough. *(Pause)* So I put the books down and decided to fall asleep. I thought, let me sleep. Just get me through the next day. I thought certain things, I really guess certain things build up in your mind, and that's it, just it: they're built up.
    It's time to take them down. Time to forget and go to sleep.
    But I couldn't. I got restless and got up. I went outside. Sat down on the steps. And I remembered how much I wanted with you. What I longed for. All those moments alone. Because I used to wake up at night. Used to wander the hills by myself. I would go out at night and try to hear all the verses in my head. The couplets. I would walk and try to write. Try to identify. I would look at trees, or a stream, and try to lose myself. I was this vehicle to lose myself. And the world I came from, my parents, my father, what they taught me was an old world. With discipline and wealth. Maturity, guilt. Realism. Which were concerns that seemed pale now. Because this was a new world. A new understanding. Which kept exploding like that in my head. Because I would stand on a hill. In the middle of the night, wide awake. I would look down. I

would see the land where we went to school. I could
see houses and the valley. And I knew, more than
anything I have ever known, I knew I was excited.
This was excitement. It was excitement to be alive,
and to have these ideas, these notions, and all these
trees, this valley to look at, and this middle of the night
with me wide awake and happy. Out walking.

(Pause)

RICHARD: Couplets.

LOUISE: Hm?

RICHARD: *(Realizing)* You wanted to write couplets.
We talked about this.

LOUISE: You remember that?

RICHARD: You had them in your head. You had
couplets. I thought it was funny. You called them
couplets. We talked about this.

(Pause)

LOUISE: What else?

RICHARD: You asked to go for a walk.

LOUISE: Which walk?

RICHARD: I don't know. It was a walk. And I said, No.
No more walks. I have a better idea. I said, I have a
motorcycle.

LOUISE: Yes. That's right.

RICHARD: I keep a motorcycle down there. I keep it
down the road.

LOUISE: Which road?

RICHARD: I don't know. I don't know the road.

LOUISE: Then how did you get it?

RICHARD: I don't remember.

LOUISE: Yes, you got it somewhere.

RICHARD: I bought it? I wasn't supposed to buy it?

LOUISE: Yes.

RICHARD: And why did I want to go on a motorcycle this particular time?

LOUISE: You scared me.

RICHARD: I wanted to scare you?

LOUISE: No. You wanted to make sure we could never, ever change.

RICHARD: We wouldn't change?

LOUISE: Yes.

RICHARD: How could I do that? How could I stop a change?

(Pause)

LOUISE: I think it's perfectly obvious how you could do that. Stop change.

(Pause)

RICHARD: I don't remember. *(Stands. He goes downstage to a window. He looks out.)* Somebody is sitting on my bench.

(LOUISE goes to a window. She looks out.)

LOUISE: Carla. Carla is sitting on your bench. *(Pause)* She's waving.

RICHARD: Hm?

LOUISE: Can you see her waving?

RICHARD: No. I didn't.

LOUISE: Well, she's waving. She looks very nice, out there, waving.

(They look out through their windows.)

LOUISE: Do you speak to her? Does she tell you things? When Carla comes in. When she visits?

RICHARD: Yes. I speak.

LOUISE: What do you talk about? The two of you.

RICHARD: She explains colonialism.

LOUISE: What?

RICHARD: She explains it to me. Colonialism.

LOUISE: Okay.

RICHARD: Malcolm Cribbs explains the universe.

LOUISE: Right.

RICHARD: Carla explains Rumania.

LOUISE: Right, she told me.

RICHARD: She was a partisan.

LOUISE: Hm?

RICHARD: A partisan. In the mountains.

LOUISE: She says that?

RICHARD: Yes. She says she fought there.

LOUISE: And did she?

RICHARD: What?

LOUISE: Did she actually fight there? What, in World War Two?

RICHARD: You don't think so?

LOUISE: Well, I don't know. I hadn't realized.

RICHARD: You think she's too foolish?

LOUISE: Foolish?

RICHARD: For fighting in the mountains, yes. Foolish.

LOUISE: I never suggested that.

RICHARD: No, she disturbs you, this woman.

LOUISE: What?

RICHARD: I have to get back to my chair. *(Heads back to his chair. He reaches it. He holds onto the chair.)*

LOUISE: Richard?

(No response)

LOUISE: Richard, I never intended, in any way, to suggest she was foolish. *(Pause)* Richard, I don't know who you're not talking to right now. Who you think is in this room now. *(Pause)* Is it Harris? Is it something Harris said when he was here before? About Carla? Or your father? Are you thinking of your father?

(RICHARD sits down in his chair.)

RICHARD: *(Apologetically)* This floor isn't very straight. *(Pause. With deliberation)* Every day I try to remember the things I did. Everything done here on earth.
But I can't.
And so I remember Carla. What she has told me. How she fought in the mountains. And I try to imagine a young woman who was captured. Taken away from her friends. And tied to a table. With men standing over. And one of them, an officer, is breaking her feet. To get her to talk.
And then I think, who am I? Did I ever fight like that, or sacrifice? To change what I thought could be changed? Did I have that kind of exuberance? *(Pause)* I am trying to remember your epiphany. All week, your epiphany, where your father died, and you went home. And your mother told you to go to the attic.

(Pause)

LOUISE: I was asked, by my mother, to go up and pack some things. Put them away in boxes. I could help that way, with the boxes. So I went up to the attic, thinking,

this is strange. Being home. And my father is dead.
There seems to be no pain. I can't feel any pain.
I'm really very blank.

   And then in the attic, I saw a chair. In the middle
of the floor by itself, a child's chair. And sitting in it
was a puppet. A marionette that I remembered hung
from the ceiling in my room. Above my bed. And then
I remembered how I could go to bed, afraid. Because
my father could be angry, or strict. And I would reach
up, from bed, and hold onto this puppet's foot. And
then I remembered how I called it Moonface. How I
imagined the two of us, this puppet and me, floating,
it was pulling me up. Taking me away. Into the
distance. Where I could rest.

   So I walked over to the puppet. And saw it had two
little shoes. I could see the laces untied. And I don't
know, I started to unhook, I think, because I sat down.
I thought, how sad, these laces are untied, who could
have left them untied, all this time probably since I was
a child? Who left this puppet here for me to see? And
I began weeping. And to stop this weeping I tied the
laces. Till I remembered my father. I had forgotten my
father gave me this puppet. And then I realized
probably my father came up. To this attic and put the
puppet here. In this chair right where I would see.

   And then it came to me. It slammed me in the chest.
He wanted to talk to me. And I stayed like that, I stayed
on the floor, holding on to the shoes. Because he
wanted to talk to me. (Pause) I became unconscious
then. Because I found myself going for a long walk.
With my father. And there was a long line of trees, an
open space, like a runway in a forest. And I don't know
what we talked about, or even if we talked, except I
could hear the word "perfect". Somebody spoke this
word "perfect" and I could hear it. My father could
hear it too. Both of us. And it made me happy, or joyful,
to see my father was perfect, and I could be too. And

then suddenly I saw no need between us. No inability to speak.

And then the next thing I knew my father was gone. And I saw my mother then. She came into the attic. And I was in the attic too. But I could still hear the word "perfect", I could still understand. And in the middle of understanding, I asked my mother, Which boxes? What boxes should I use? And what else might I do? To help her?

Then later she must have left, and I fell asleep. And when I woke up, I couldn't understand what happened. I thought, something has happened. So I went downstairs to ask my mother what happened.

And she seemed peaceful, my mother. She said, Nothing much. You were kind, Louise. You were very kind up there. In the attic. *(Pause)* I can tell you, however, I have never spoken to anyone like that. Been so gentle, or loved anyone like that, in my life. As I loved my mother because she happened to come into the attic. She happened to walk in when I understood the word "perfect".

(Pause)

RICHARD: *(To himself)* Kind. Your mother said kind. *(Reaches into a pocket)*

LOUISE: You remember it?

(RICHARD *takes out a photograph. He looks at it. He holds it out to* LOUISE.)

LOUISE: *(Taking it)* This is the picture? Where we stood together? *(Pause)* I can't see my face. It's overexposed.

RICHARD: Practice.

LOUISE: What?

RICHARD: I practiced on a motorcycle. I practiced a lot.

LOUISE: Yes?

(Pause)

RICHARD: I paid somebody in town. To let me keep it in town. And I used to sneak down and ride it. It was a secret even from you. Because the first thing I wanted to do in my life was to play soccer. To go to Europe and play soccer. On an Italian team. But there was a second thing growing. Which was to ride a motorcycle. To race it. *(Pause)* And when I took you on the motorcycle, it was this night. In the photograph. I think it was the photograph, later. And I didn't plan to go so fast. I started fast, but that was just showing off. I was showing what I practiced. That's all. And you knew that too. Because I could feel you trusting me. You were trusting and holding onto my back. Like my back was broad. It was a big wall, a protection, between you and anything that could happen to you no matter what was ahead of us in this world. And there was nothing that could equal the feeling. The trust I felt you had in me.

And then I found these grooves in my mind. I had been looking for these grooves. And I put my mind in each groove and it took us up and down the mountain, the mountain roads, like a centripetal force. Everything was guided. It was in a groove. But then I began to understand there is an edge to each groove. *(Rises from his chair)* You can go to an even further edge. And I wanted so bad to go to this edge. I wanted to step off. Because I saw this edge in front of us and I knew we could step off. I knew we could do it together.

And then I felt you. I felt you slamming your head into my back. I could hear you pulling on my hair with your hand and screaming to me to stop. I felt you ripping the skin of my cheek off. *(Pause)* And I think it was a miracle we did stop. That the bike flew away from my legs, and my hands, it left my control. And we slid on my back, somehow up a hill.

But that changed me. And it changed you. Because you knew I could kill you. And I would kill myself. You could see this hole. You knew I could go down the hole. *(Sinks to the floor)* That's why I remember your face. I remember when we got up from the motorcycle. And you looked at me from your face. *(Pause)* So this is me now. I'm in a room now. And I think all the things I did before I came to this room were just a trick. To take up time. Make activity. A trick that didn't work to keep from coming to this room. *(Pause)* Because this is my room. A white room. I have belonged in this room. I have belonged to come to a place where walls can move, and nothing is even. *(Pause)* What I don't think belongs to me. What I didn't know. Was that you could visit. You could still visit. Even after you saw.

And I am very grateful. You cannot know. You cannot know, how after all these things, I did not know we could still have this visit.

(Pause. LOUISE *steps behind* RICHARD. *She kneels down and embraces him from behind, her arms across his chest. They look out front.)*

LOUISE: If you wanted. I would trust you again.

RICHARD: Trust me how?

LOUISE: I will trust we can make it out of here. Both of us. To that bench.

*(*CARLA *appears at the door. She looks transformed.)*

CARLA: You saw me?

LOUISE: Yes. We saw.

CARLA: You saw me waving? You know why I waved?

LOUISE: I guess you saw us.

CARLA: No. I didn't see you.

LOUISE: We were looking out.

CARLA: No. I waved at something else.

LOUISE: Oh?

CARLA: Before, yeah, I realized it was you.

LOUISE: You thought we were something else?

CARLA: Just a lady. That's all.

LOUISE: What lady?

(CARLA *steps into the room. She sits down.*)

CARLA: Do you think I look nice?

LOUISE: Hm?

CARLA: How nice am I looking?

LOUISE: Very nice. I agree. Are those new?

CARLA: My slippers?

LOUISE: Yes. They have glass on them. Glass beads or something.

CARLA: I think they're pretty.

LOUISE: Your hair too. Your hair is pretty.

CARLA: Yeah. Thank you.

LOUISE: You must have really brushed your hair.

CARLA: I found a brush, yeah.

(RICHARD *gets up. He moves across the room.*)

CARLA: That's our friend.

LOUISE: (*Getting up*) Yes.

CARLA: A good person, our friend. He keeps moving these days.

LOUISE: Uh huh. (*Pause*) So what lady? Tell me, what lady were you actually waving at?

(*Pause*)

CARLA: In my mind, the breezes were so nice, out there, and the sun, I became like a little girl. I became excited. My legs, on the bench, became like little feet, which couldn't touch the ground. And I could hear my voice again. A little voice laughing. And then before my eyes, I couldn't believe it, I saw a clown. He had big red shoes and I laughed when he jumped out of the cannon. And then behind the clown, I saw a bear which was traipsing. A lion too. And somebody had an eagle riding on the back of a leopard. I could see a whole circus out there which came to town when I was just a girl. And up above was a platform. And I thought, who is standing on the platform? And then I saw a lady. She was out walking on a wire. And I thought that must be me. Sometime when I am a woman. I will know how to walk like that. But then I looked down at my hands, I could feel something cutting in my hands. And when I looked down I saw my hands were old, but I held a wire. In my hands was the other end of the wire. And then I saw the lady coming down closer to me. And so I held with all my strength, until finally this lady, she came down. She sat down on the bench next to me. And she said, Hello. We have met before. And I said, Yes, I know. And she said, I saw you when you were a child, and then I saw you when you were a young woman and the enemy captured you. And I said, I remember each time. So she said, And now, I see you are here. How do you like it here? And I said, It's okay. It's been okay. But I'm getting ready soon to leave. And she said, Good. I'll meet you again. When it's time to leave. *(Pause)* There are many people, all generations, each one, who can say they were exuberant.

LOUISE: *(Softly)* I know that.

(Pause)

CARLA: *(To* RICHARD*)* How about you, my friend? Do you know that?

RICHARD: Yes. I know that.

(Lights begin to dim. A thin dark line appears across the floor.)

CARLA: Good. Next time I will know it too. She has told me.

(CARLA is standing on the thin dark line. She holds out a hand to LOUISE and another out to RICHARD.)

(Blackout)

END OF PLAY